Copyright 2021 by Murdoch Children's Research Institute
All rights reserved. This book or any portion thereof
may not be reproduced or used in any manner whatsoever
without the express written permission of the publisher
except for the use of brief quotations in a book review.

ABN 21 006 566 9782

Address: Murdoch Children's Research Institute
Royal Children's Hospital
Flemington Road, Parkville Victoria 3052 Australia
Email: hello@sleepwithkip.com
Website: www.sleepwithkip.com

Hello! Thanks for choosing a Kip book.

Based on over two decades of research, these books are here to help your child (and you) manage some common sleep problems children have.

There's loads of advice out there about how to help children sleep, and at the Murdoch Children's Research Institute in Melbourne, Australia, we pride ourselves on generating and sharing the advice you need based on evidence and research. This advice is now captured in the Kip books.

This series of six books is all about the common sleep problems in children, how your child can help themselves tackle them, and how you can manage them. Most are what we call 'behavioural' sleep problems (like getting to sleep, waking up overnight or waking up early).

As a paediatrician and researcher, I have seen over my 20 year journey, how much of an impact poor sleep in babies and children had on them as well as their parents. I met so many parents who were desperate for a good night's sleep! So I hope you find this book fun and helpful, for you, your child, your family and your friends.

Enjoy and sleep well!
Prof Harriet Hiscock

A Beach in THE BEDROOM

and **tossed** and **turned.**

'You're making a **lot of noise,**' said Kip, **looking up** from a **book.**

'I feel **all tight**, **tense** and **itchy**.'

'I just **can't** relax.'

'Well, why don't we build a beach?'

'Build a beach?'

'Yes! Build a beach. A perfect beach for you to relax.'

'What would you like **your beach to have?**'

'Hmm...nice soft sand.'

'I want **cool, blue water.** The **kind** that **swirls your hair around** as you **float** in it.'

'What next? What next?'

'Can I get a **soft, salty breeze** on **my face?**'

'What next? What next?'

'Well, a beach **needs a towel.**'

'What next?
What next?'

BWUURRRRRRR

'Hear that **sound?** That's **Boddington,** our very best, **nicest whale.**'

close your eyes,
and enjoy your beach.'

'My very own beach.'

Sweet Snoozing -Kip!

Visual imagery and relaxation technique
A Beach in the Bedroom

Worry can be a big problem when it comes to getting to sleep. Especially as children get older. But relaxation techniques and visualisation can help take their minds off these worries. This story can help get them started as they imagine they are lying on the beach, with the sound of waves lapping the shore and a warm breeze passing over them.

This is a technique best suited to children aged four years and up, and best used at a time other than bedtime to start with. We don't want them getting worried about the technique working, which can happen if they start learning it at bedtime. Start perhaps on the floor of the bedroom in the afternoon. When this technique works, you'll find children start to use it naturally before bedtime.

Oh, and it's best not to ask a child about their day just before bedtime. If things haven't gone so well, this may upset them. Try talking about the day in the afternoon or at dinner time.

Also available in the Kip book series

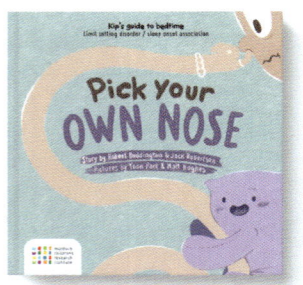

Pick your Own Nose

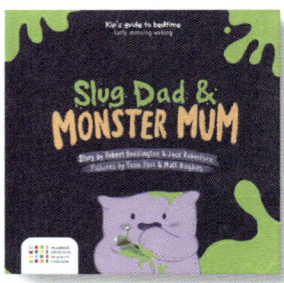

Slug Dad & Monster Mum

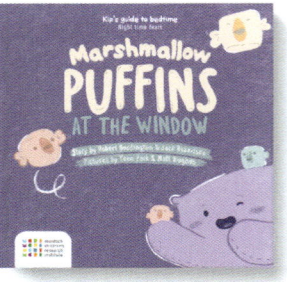

Marshmallow Puffins at the Window

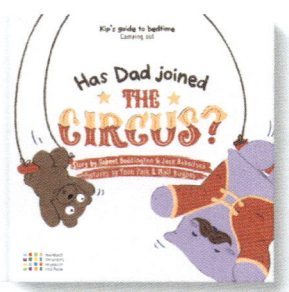

Has Dad joined the Circus?

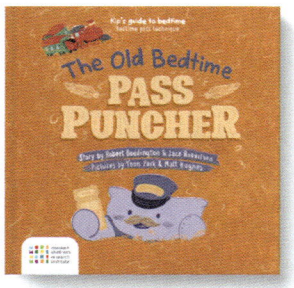

The Old Bedtime Pass Puncher

Murdoch Children's Research Institute is a not-for-profit organisation and the largest child health research institute in Australia. Their dedicated team of more than 1200 talented researchers is united to better understand, prevent and treat childhood conditions, helping to give all children the opportunity to live healthy and fulfilled lives.

For more than 35 years, the Murdoch Children's has been leading collaborations with national and international partners, policymakers, and health practitioners, to ensure that the benefits of its research are translated into real therapies and policies that improve the health and wellbeing of children all around the world, from preconception through to early adulthood.

Be sure to check out our website www.sleepwithkip.com and do the free Child Sleep Check to see what types of sleep problems your child may be experiencing and how you might be best able to help them.

Printed in Great Britain
by Amazon